Private Investigation School: 15 Valuable Skills That Will Help You Fast-Track Your Career In Investigation

by Sean Abraham

Thank you for getting my book!

The link below contains information on how to get your license.

Private Investigator License

Become a subscriber to my website and stay in the know about new books and posts coming up

Sean Abraham

Copyright © 2019-2020 by Sean's Network
www.seansnetwork.com

All rights reserved. No part of this publication may be reproduced, distributed, or transmitted in any form or by any means including photocopying, recording, or other electronic or mechanical methods, without the prior written permission of the publisher, except in the case of brief quotations embodied in reviews and certain other non commercial uses permitted by copyright law.

While all attempts have been made to verify the information provided in this publication, neither the author, not the publisher assumes any responsibility for errors, omissions, or contrary interpretations on the subject matter herein. This book is for informational purposes only. The views expressed are those of the audience alone, and should not be taken as expert instructions or commands. No guarantees for earnings or any other results - of any kind - are being made by the author or publisher, nor are any liabilities being assumed. The reader is entirely responsible for his or her actions.

All products recommended have been tested by the author. Readers or purchasers are advised to do their research before making any purchase online. No guarantees of earnings or other results - of any kind - nor any liability is assumed for the publisher or author. The reader is entirely responsible for his or her actions.

Adherence to all applicable laws and regulations, including international, federal, state, and local governing professional licensing, business practices, advertising, and all other aspects of doing business in the US, Canada, or any other jurisdiction is the sole responsibility of the reader or purchaser. Neither the author nor the publisher assumes any responsibility whatsoever on the behalf of the purchaser or reader of these materials. Any perceived slight of any individual or organization is purely unintentional.

sean.abraham@seansnetwork.com

Sean Abraham, is the founder of Sean's Network, a platform that helps people in business consulting in investigation education, cruise line industry, and franchise business.

Sean has had experience in franchising his own business, maneuvering the complex corporate tax system, including bookkeeping, successful budget marketing to become the only franchise business to retain sales beyond the other franchises surpassing them by up to 11%.

Sean enjoys typically working on a cruise and travel to see places that he would not have thought about visiting.

In the exploration of his next goal of becoming a Digital Nomad, Sean decided to pass his experience and expertise in the field into a written format to help people alike pursue a rewarding career and ultimately the freedom that comes with it.

CHAPTER ONE

Investigating Senses

Do you have an observant and discreet demeanor? Do you get excited when people say that they didn't notice you were there the whole time? (in the right way not in an anti-social way!). Then you have a knack to blend into the background, and you can pay attention to the surroundings, just need a bit of practice and awareness and you will be on your way to become an investigator.

Focus On Being Observant

Being an observer means so much more than just watching. It is also paying attention. Means you can observe a person's demeanor and can tell his next behavior. You can gather invaluable information and predict the next movement. This will increase your awareness of the person. If you can see the other person's motives and they don't tell you with his or her own words, that can make a difference. So from now on, pay attention to details of the surroundings and see why certain things are placed the way they are, why certain people act the way they do.

Pay Attention

In paying attention, you may start training your sub-conscious, and this will encourage the behavior to become a habit. That would mean that your investigation senses will always be on overdrive. People may even compliment you on how well you remember specific details and could be a conversation turner as well. Give it a try, but remember, forming a habit takes time and consistency.

Actionable Observation

There are also ways to observe a situation by being involved in the case. Sometimes an intervention is necessary because you know that the situation demands it. Have you ever said something or did something just to see the other person's reaction? Or to that effect? It just means you have a curious mind, and you want to observe the behavior or outcome of specific actions. Because for every effort, there is an unusual reaction. Okay, fine, I changed that sentence a bit from Newton's Law of Motion.

Detail Observer

Physical evidence through observation is convincing as well in the world of investigation. If you are detailed oriented, you will notice the little things like if a wedding ring was taken off, smoker, etc. You will learn to implement this in a narrative record keeping. This means you will use video footage, audio recordings, or field notes as a means necessary to retain the information as it happens. You can learn more about that through your training as you progress in the field.

CHAPTER TWO

Overlooking Is A Mistake

Details, Details, Details

These cannot be emphasized as they are the cause of making a difference in a case you are working on. The aspect of the weather could make the situation turn, like visibility during that particular time.

Also, sometimes, these details can be connected to other cases where another event occurred. Possibly, the additional investigators' notes were not as good as yours and did not include specific information. These can be about the weather, noise, dog barking, crying kid, or anything that could be used to help the case.

Expertise In The Field

Even if you think these details are not as important. Possibly to a Subject Matter Expert (SME) could benefit them in making an expert decision in the court of law. Of course, this does not need to be a subject matter expert in many cases. It can also be that the dog was barking due to a presence in the area. This could determine the route of a burglar or direction of escape. Write as much detail as possible, it could help later during the investigation. Even if you think the aspect was not significant at that time.

CHAPTER THREE

Best Managing Practices

How does an investigator take care of themselves? Without a doubt, they need to be mentally fit to undertake cases.

To create a practice, investigators will need to manage themselves to continue for a long career without impacting their abilities to perform.

If you face barriers in working as an investigator, look into ways of coping with them. The everyday stresses that you may experience as an investigator can be suppressed.

Teamwork Makes The Dream Work

If you are part of an organization, a meeting every 2 weeks to discuss current matters will benefit you. As an investigator, you are usually working alone. There are alternatives like combining the minds of other people within the organization that can help you distribute better ideas and perform the task within a shorter time-frame.

Not to mention managing your contribution to being part of a team that can contribute to solutions and brainstorm ideas.

Talking To Improve

As investigators, we see and hear things that could be distressing. Some repeat the scenarios in their mind and have no one to discuss with. As part of the solution, sometimes talking to colleagues may alleviate the continuous mental pictures encountered during a case. The daunting task to forget is a process for some and one that can be cured with talking.

Any work that we undertake can cause temporary pain as we are humans, and emotions can eventually get in the way. That's why the suggestion of talking through your problems will help. If needed, you can also hire professional help if you believe the need is there.

Beauty Sleep

As investigators, you may face a block and unsure of where to take the next step. Sleep on the problem and think of it with a rested mind. You may find a different approach that could guide you in the right solution.

Some have found that through sleep, we wake up with a solution already. So avoid going from task to task as this can affect your profound thinking ability.

Have Fun While Learning

Learning can be fun. Undertake a topic that could benefit your career. If you find that the problem is annoying or not for you, give the subject a more relaxed approach. You can do this before diving into the more complex topics.

People say that they don't like to read, but if you start off with easy books, then you will automatically keep progressing to the more complex ones. Give it a try, and you might find yourself a new hobby or end up learning something new.

Diversion, Distractions, Then Solutions

Investigation in itself can be consuming. Doing the same thing may keep you on the game, but from time to time, practice different things. Having too much of one thing can get stale.

Find yourself a hobby to diversify your persona. The range is unlimited from reading, sports, self-improvement, cooking, etc. Dodge being a full-time investigator and learn different skills.

Working For The Weekends

Avoid working weekends, if possible. Some investigators are supposed to work 7 days a week, 12 hour days until the case is over. If possible, avoid the weekend as this will help you rest your body and refresh your brain. Investigators write a lot, and this can be good practice as it will help you accomplish tasks better. When you are well-rested and take your focus to another area in your life, other aspects of life improve.

Productive Breaks

Taking breaks in between work, researchers find that this is very helpful as it increases productivity. When you give yourself a few minutes away from the screen, you can come back and continue. You will notice an improvement and possibly improve and polish the work that you were doing.

Limit Yourself

Finding yourself at your limits? If you find yourself overworked, don't take on more projects. Learn to say no to colleagues, clients, lawyers, co-workers without impacting the relationship.

Your passion for your job should stay intact but not at the price of your health. That's why if you find yourself at your limits, get a break and recharge.

The longer you go without a break the longer it will take you to recuperate from your daily grind. If you don't find your breaktime, then divise fancy ways to give yourself the rest you need.

CHAPTER FOUR
Organized Mess

Being a Private Eye means you need to keep your life organized. There is no such thing as a rushed job, as anything you do may end up in the eyes of a lawyer for scrutiny.

Write As Your Life Depends On It

That being said, your notes must be concise to paint the picture as you will later be asked to recollect all the information gathered into chronological order. This means that you have to remember all the news while you read your own notes. You also have to be able to explain that to someone in an organized, transparent manner. In some instances, you will need to be court ready to speak about your investigation. Keep your handwriting neat and legible. You can practice printing your notes to avoid them being unreadable. We can leave that for the doctors to scribble, but for investigators, keep it readable.

Organization Matters

Being organized can save you time and in turn, give you an edge to be prepared for unexpected occasions. This could mean that when you are doing surveillance and using video footage, you have a system where you will not run out of battery life. This can be accomplished by bringing an extra supply or a power source that can connect to your car to recharge during the downtime quickly. Always be prepared to use your equipment, notes, vehicles, and other gadgets that will facilitate your job as a Private Investigator.

CHAPTER FIVE

Dependable Adult

Still living in mom's basement? That's nothing to do with the topic but puts things into perspective on independence.

When you are a Private Investigator, you will have to work alone and in some cases, depending on a budget of the operation with limited equipment. Some agencies will provide you with all the tools and equipment. Meanwhile, others, you will need everything from scratch.

There will be cases that will require you to have the car, video equipment, notes, and hotel if necessary. There are Private Investigator companies that fly you to other provinces, states, or even countries, depending on how large a firm is. Keep in mind that in these cases, they will provide compensation accordingly.

Adapting Seamlessly

You will have to start adapting to your environment, whichever that may be. If you are following someone, you will need to blend into the surroundings without attracting attention. You will have to anticipate paying to get into trains, subways, buses, taxis, amusement parks, and other places. Wherever the subject takes you to keep track of them and not lose them. Keep a supply of cash handy and some sort of company or personal credit card.

You will need to rely on yourself and nobody else. Focusing on the most essential tasks, following, understanding the boundaries, taking risks, and depending on yourself to navigate the city with ease.

Risk For Adventure

Private Investigation does have its risks, and no situation should be taken lightly, keeping your guard up at all times is necessary for survival and safety. Keep your senses on alert and avoid being dependent as much as possible.

Be proactive, not reactive.

CHAPTER SIX

Keeping Guard

Practicing discretion as a Private Investigator can mean the difference in your reputation for a long and prosperous career, and you will be in demand. Avoid making the mistake of discussing your work with other people who are not privileged to other people's information.

Be Secretive

The job you have chosen is based on discretion, as this information can be sensitive if the word gets out. Once that happens, there is no going back to redeem your reputation. This could cause a significant setback and possibly land you in some trouble. The latter does not happen often but just putting it out there to avoid making a mistake. Treat it like your mistress. A secret locked away with no reason for anyone to know.

Dependability

People rely on you to complete the task they entrusted you with. So when a case comes to you, and you are unsure if you can finish, let the other person know so that you are not just making empty promises.

That being said, there have been investigators who have not completed tasks. These have had people complain to the registrar, who, in turn, has given some hefty ultimatums.

Handle Yourself

Later in this book, we will discuss Privacy Law as well. This is so that you may have some background sense of what it means to be discreet when handling sensitive information.

CHAPTER SEVEN

Career Options

So you still want to be an investigator? Here you can explore the opportunities provided in this field. It definitely has a few options to choose from, depending on your desired niche.

Finding Your Niche

What is it all about? Mostly Private Investigators are people who are trained to gather information and evidence. There are many approaches one can pick in the field of choice. Options vary but can be in surveillance, undercover assignments, or using a computer to do background information research. Mainly you will collect and present the information and evidence in a way to satisfy judges, lawyers, detectives, and anyone that may find the information useful.

The list here will provide the assignments related to Investigation:

- Financial Investigation
- Tracing Assets
- Process Serving
- Missing Persons
- Law-related Investigations
- Background Investigations
- Information Search
- Domestic Law
- Family Law Matters
- Slips & Falls
- Motor Vehicle Accidents
- Workplace Accidents

- Insurance Claims
- Accident Investigations
- Theft Investigations
- Loss Prevention
- Commercial Investigations
- Criminal Defense Investigations
- Undercover Investigations

Let's explore the range of opportunities one can pursue as a Private Investigator within the following industries:

#1 Private Investigation Companies (Of Course!)

#2 Law firms

#3 Insurance Companies

#4 Retail Chains

#5 Corporate Security Departments

#6 Independent Private Investigators

The first one entails being hired through an agency that will then, in turn, provide you with cases to be investigated. They can range from surveillance, domestic investigations, insurance fraud, corporate investigations cases, and they depend on your skillset. The accumulated experience will determine where you will be placed accordingly. Some instances require training or experience, and not all employers feel comfortable putting an under trained investigator in a case they cannot complete. Plenty of opportunities will get you there, patience, my friend.

Second and third, if you find work for a law firm or insurance company, you will be conducting research, interviewing witnesses, gathering evidence. Most of the time, you will be analyzing data and building cases for the employer. Usually, insurance companies can provide a good source of steady income.

Fourth, retail chains will advertise for Loss Prevention Officers to target theft in their respective places of business. They trust the Private Investigator to protect their assets. That being said, you will most likely be undercover to check if employees are stealing company property or if the customers are stealing.

When a customer usually steals, the Loss Prevention Officer will call the police if they believe the perpetrator can become aggressive, deceptive, or is carrying a weapon. So the suggestion is safety first.

Some of these retail chains depend on the evidence gathered to determine the root cause of their losses. Feels rewarding after helping your employer. Still, you can't help to feel bad for the employee who is stealing from the very place that provides him or her a living.

Fifth, these will be your giant tech companies, financial companies, banks, sports organizations, entertainment organizations, transportation companies, and logistics companies. All of which require a Private Investigator to be their corporate safety, security, and loss prevention officer.

Lastly, the independent investigator, usually most people's ultimate step into their career to start his or her own company. Being your own boss, you can choose to take cases on your strengths or whichever type of situations you like to be in, all up to you.

The choices of being your own boss are unlimited within the field. You can choose to hire your own Private Investigators to complete cases, which in this instance you can concentrate on other matters.

Owning your own company does give you the freedom to have choices. It will also be a lot of work in the beginning to establish a reputation as the service provider that your clientele will come to trust you to undertake.

There you have it, of course, if you do find a niche that is not listed here, you can definitely feel free to pursue it. The job of an investigator has a wide variety of options and avenues. You may do your own exploring and soul searching to figure out which one of these you will apply yourself in and become a Subject Matter Expert(SME) one day.

CHAPTER EIGHT

Investigation Branch

As private Investigators, we have limitations to what we can do and what we cannot do. To put things into perspective, an Investigator is much like any other civilian, with good knowledge of the law and its application in certain situations.

So what is this all about?

To start the reason to understand this section of the Private Investigator is so that we act within our rights.

We will discuss Privacy Law as this has been known to confuse people, confused me for sure. This is determined by the nature of the organization handling personal information. Like which level of government the information is protected under. The federal government, provincial, territorial, private, commercial, federally regulated, location, type of information, and if the info crosses states or provinces.

As you can see, this could cause someone to get confused and ponder which one to listen to. Let's simplify a bit.

When referring to Personal information Data, we mean an identifiable individual. A combination of data or data on its own that can identify the individual through that information.

Consider the following pieces that can identify an individual, stay with me, race, ethnic origin, religion, age, marital status, medical, education, employment history, financial information, DNA, opinions about the person from other people. These combined or on their own can pinpoint or assist in identifying an individual.

If you have information that a person works in a particular establishment, that information is not considered identifiable. This is because the person cannot be linked with that kind of information. Other more certain information needs to be in place.

Public servants have their information public, meaning that their data is general knowledge and can be given out, such as their name position and title.

If you are interested in finding someone's information, there are two ways to freely find this. One is if the person works for a charity group or has a political party association. Within these circumstances you can identify a person. This does not apply to universities, schools, and hospitals.

So you might ask what about banks? Yes, there is a Bank Act that the government has placed a regulation in place. They like to know your money matters. Financial institutions need to disclose your financial information to the government.

Tools To Build

So you may ask, what are the ways to get around such complicated laws? Well, the answer is quite simple, in this modern age, we have tools to help us find a vast majority of information.

People, for the most part, are creatures that love to interact with one another. In some instances, this helps the investigator. They will be displaying pictures or check-in to places on social media, and this will be published on the world wide web for friends and Private Investigators to see. Well, that last part not really for them, but unknowingly placing information online will eventually get found.

Also, you may say, but pictures are okay, right? Well, when you take photos with a GPS enabled gadget, which is most of them nowadays, the image contains a location. That's how sometimes Facebook can tell the location of your picture and tell you to check-in to nearby areas.

Improvise

If you are looking to get information from someone but can't seem to... what do you do? You improvise! Well, here are some ways to receive information depending on the type of information you are gathering:

- Creating a promotion that entices the person to provide his or her information. Freely!

- If you find multiple addresses for one person, you can call or send a letter to see which one is not returned. You can also use the same method, entice for the individual to give his or her information freely. This can be through contest participation (can be a real one too).

- Use a social media account to communicate with the organization or individual.

- If times are tough and you are trying to reach someone who is always surrounded by security, create a persona that will serve as undercover for the company. If process serving is your goal, then you will be close enough to eventually catch the person. It takes time and persistence.

- Missing person? Try to go through family and friends, sometimes they can unknowingly provide keys to getting closer to where they are. If they don't budge, surveillance outside the properties might do the trick. Only if you believe they visit the area.

Network

If you are stuck and can't find a way to crack your case or that piece of information. Join a group of like-minded people and find ways to work through some stubborn investigations. There is a lot of talent in the world, and that talent is accessible.

Overall if someone does not want to get found, then they will take all precautions to do so. If what they have to lose is worth hiding for, then they will do a great job at it. Don't get discouraged, roadblocks happen. Then we go onto new cases and better situations.

Differences

Police Officers and Private Investigators are not the same. One is considered a Peace Officer for the general public, and the Private Investigator works for the private sector. Also, they both don't have the same powers.

If you choose the Private Investigator route, you cannot make an official arrest. Citizens arrest only. Police Officers can get a warrant, arrest suspects, and enforce the law. You will work alone and rarely part of a team. So get used to it now.

CHAPTER NINE

Managing The Work

Case Law

"In deciding which is the better rule, the legal writer may also examine what the majority of other courts have held and what the trend seems to be."

The quote is basically using other court causes from the past when a similar case can be used for the current one. The legal term is Case Law.

We will look at some summary scenarios. These will help with understanding the type of events that could occur during a career in the investigation industry. Not to mention, these circumstances do arise, and having the answer would be great.

Tribes, Indians, & Aboriginals

A tribal court has the same enforcements as the regular court. So a restraining order or any tribal judge order is valid.

A man is driving without proper registration in the Indian Territory. As per law, a civil action cannot be taken against the driver. The only measure that can be made in these territories are criminal in nature.

On the other hand, a tribal enforcer would have authority over civil matters within the territory.

Keep in mind that everything you do might end up in court one day.

Workplace Incidents

We will look at a more in-depth scenario that would apply to the workplace investigation and how to conduct research.

If you have a person, who has fallen off a ladder and hurts his back.

It seems like a simple case, but the document would contain a few things.

Exploring the environmental conditions like weather conditions, type of surface, the incline of the ladder, if the surface is slippery, and how stable the ladder actually is.

Also, it might be a good idea to take pictures as well and be able to answer about the condition of the ladder. Other aspects to check are inspecting the cleanliness of the ladder. The height of the ladder compared to where the individual was trying to reach. Additionally, How much load was taken with the person on the ladder, including the weight of the person.

The injured person would need to be interviewed by asking.

- How/she feels
- What are the injuries
- Asking what happened
- What were you trying to do
- Was the person holding onto anything
- Was this the only ladder
- Was there a different way to accomplish the same job
- Has the employee gone through safety training?
- Was the positioning of the ladder the safest.
- Was anyone available to stabilize the ladder?
- Was the ladder checked before using it?

Other people that were in the area they could answer some of the questions to complete the incident.

Also, other research about the ladder itself like the inspection of the ladder.

If you can question scenarios just by looking at them and find the answers, then you can investigate situations.

As mentioned in the beginning, see each place that you visit and investigate the site. Pay attention to details, and the habit will become easier to adopt.

Computer Hackers

This one involves a business corporation that has been attacked by cybercrime.

The owner is being asked to give $500,000 within 72 hours to avoid leaking information.

The owner has the choice to pay the ransom or hire an expert agency to secure the data.

Both have consequences, and the best ethical thing to do is to hire the agency to fight cybercrime.

The reason for this would be to avoid future crimes by reinforcing the firewall against such crimes against the company.

By not funding the criminals as a large sum of money could negatively benefit the same company or others in the same position.

By hiring the cybercrime agency, you may even bring the criminal to justice by finding his or her identity.

Rule Of Law

In context, it is better to be ruled by law than to be ruled by leaders who can act any way they like. If a king or dictator rules the people, then they are exercising power without guidelines.

The laws apply to everyone, including the leaders.

If a law needs changing, then this can be accomplished as well in a peaceful manner.

The same goes for the enforcers of the law. We cannot produce evidence as the consequences can end you in disciplinary action, charged with a crime, or lose your job.

CHAPTER TEN

Evidence Gathering

Do you know how to speak to an individual with compassion, tact, and confidence?

The skills to take interviews are crucial to obtain the information targeted to the case at hand. The solution and case prosecution depend on it.

Accuracy is difficult to obtain to get the full picture of the situation that occurred.

In the past, interviews were aimed to lead the witness. This was done by suggestion and reinforcement at the end of the question.

For example, "he was wearing a blue shirt, wasn't he?" "So, he was running from the police, right?"

Thereby, the interviewer should not be asking many questions. The witness should not be interrupted if a story or narrative is being freely given by the witness.

With an inexperienced interviewer, you run a high risk of inaccurate answers to the questions and the narrative changes due to suggestions imposed by the interviewer or his opinion.

Tactical Interview

Forensic research scientists have developed interviewing skills better suited in such situations that trigger a higher accuracy delivered by the witness.

A good interviewer who possesses experience through practice or skills acquired through education will automatically implement them in the interview. The following list is created to retrieve information from a witness efficiently.

- The methods will have an increased amount of information.
- Decrease the amount of recalling an event incorrectly.
- Developing rapport with the witness.
- Asking open-ended questions.
- Asking neutral questions, thereby avoiding leading and/or suggestive problems.
- Interviewing with the broader aspects of the narrative then narrowing down the details at the end.

By following these, you will notice significantly more information gathered than standard question and answer type of interviews.

Psychology Says

Psychologically there are three processes. Memory & cognition, social dynamics, and communication. All who utilize the non-verbal and verbal modes of expression.

The interviewer will need to adapt in specific scenarios rather than following a rigid template of questions. If the situation demands a more detailed answer, the interviewer can change his or her approach.

Each interviewer should be prepared to change by adapting to the situation the interview takes them.

Let's explore the routine step by step, but as explained, this can be modified depending upon the situation.

- An introduction is made to establish rapport between interviewer and witness. The social expectation will be determined based on the presentation with the witness. Aiming to be a witness centered approached.

- The opportunity to narrate the full story voluntarily without interruption. During this time, you can construct a strategy to ask further questions to clarify and enhance the accuracy of the report.

- The witness will then need to be guided through a rich-memory representation of his narrative.

- Then review the information along with the witness by concentrating on all the details.

- Closing the interview with all the background detail of the witness. Providing your contact information for if the witness recalls any additional information.

Witness Versus Interviewer

Some witnesses are uncomfortable to openly narrate the information because they are involved in a personal situation and don't feel comfortable telling this to a stranger. Rapport with the witness comes in handy here.

During such situations, your rapport with the witness will need to be initiated. A comfortable environment will be beneficial to be established before commencing the interview.

80-20 Rule

The interviewer can establish that the witness is in charge of telling the story, and the involvement of the interviewer will be around 20%.

Statement taking is more than just taking notes, do you have the ability to keep your writing factual, without opinion, without filler language, and keep it understandable?

Statement taking week-long courses have been introduced to become good at this skill.

So what are these used for?

Statements are taken to paint the picture of the situation described by the person at that particular time. They are used during investigations, and the person who gave the statement does not need to be present during the trial.

Statements are valuable pieces of information that can assist in refreshing the memory in court.

Statements can also determine and assess witnesses' consistency. In this instance, the witness' testimonial during court can be checked and cross-examined if inconsistencies are present.

Written Records

Written information supersedes witnesses' oral information given during the time in court.

Consented Recording

Audio recording can assist in capturing more details that can be eventually integrated into the statement for a better and detailed report.

Statement Do's

If you have written statements or just getting started, you can refer to this page and keep these points in mind to keep the mind frame towards an excellent report.

- Write the report in the first person and past tense.
- Use chronological order to the best of your ability. If you find that something does not fit in order, then review the report.
- Use the active voice; this is easier to read.
- No matter how the report looks, always check punctuation and spelling of the full story. Mistakes can be easy targets against you in a trial.
- Avoid jargon and words that are not easily understandable.
- Organize the report with openings, paragraphs, and headings.
- Choose the appropriate words to describe the incident.
- Avoid opinions and concentrate on writing facts.

You, as the Private Investigator, will regularly write reports of occurrences. These are comprehensive reports of the duties and tasks of the observances.

Reports are objective and standardized. Insurance and legal reports have their layout, and you will be provided with it to fill in the story.

All reports include the basics, the date, time, location, action, behaviors, description of the people, observations, time of completion of the story, and other information which is deemed to be essential.

CHAPTER ELEVEN

Evidence Handling

Why is collecting the evidence necessary? Why can the obvious not be simply understood? How come some evidence is not admissible? Many of these questions that you might have will be covered within this chapter of the book.

Evidence handling is vital as the proof that it provides in each case can be a determining factor for conviction.

We will discuss trace evidence, biological evidence, clothing evidence, injury to the body, keeping the evidence secure, and factors to follow when collecting the evidence.

Guilty or innocent?

You, as the Private Investigator can secure that decision depending on the proper handling of the evidence collection.

Your job should you wish to accept it, is to collect, package, secure, correctly maintain the evidence, then release to Law Enforcement following a strict chain of custody rules. The evidence then, can be analyzed and used for legal proceedings.

When you collect evidence, you must wear gloves at all times and change them often. Following the techniques will ensure minimal cross-contamination or degradation of DNA.

Trace evidence

Trace evidence consists of debris, like dirt, soil, gravel, grass, leaves, twigs, adhesives and tape, fibers, glass, or bullet fragments.

When collecting trace evidence, the following will assist in collection.

- Document and photograph the evidence.
- Properly secure by placing inside a paper bag or envelope.
- Seal or tape the paper bag or pouch.
- Initial the container, date it and put a time stamp across the sealed area.
Label the bag with identifying information.
- Place your signature, date the envelope, and place a time stamp on the container.

Biological evidence

Biological evidence consists of blood, skin, hair, semen, saliva, and urine.

When collecting biological evidence, the following will assist in collection.

- Cotton tip applicators can be used for buccal, oral, skin, fingernail, bite marks, perineal, vaginal, cervical Os, penile, scrotum, and rectal residue.
- The hair would be placed in an envelope.
- Use the same process as trace evidence for packaging, securing, and maintaining the evidence.

Clothing Evidence

The collection of clothing that is worn by an individual contains physical and/or biological evidence that must be preserved.

You can determine if the clothing was worn during the crime, then all the garments can be used for evidence. As the dress may contain traces of evidence like gun powder, blood, saliva, DNA, or sand or dust.

If you are researching a sexual assault case then and the clothes were not present during the crime, then undergarments can be used to check fluids for analysis.

The evidence you collect for clothing must be dried if wet or damp. Each piece of clothing separately labeled and identified with a label.

The clothes may contain tears or rips, and these also will need to be documented.

Once you have completed those steps, you will hand these over to Law Enforcement, who will send the item for further analysis at a forensic lab.

Injury To The Body

To document injury to the body, the areas that have the damage must be photographed and a diagram for the specific age pointing at the areas of the injury.

You will have to make sure you use correct terminology if filling out these body diagrams.

For example, cuts and lacerations have two different meanings. Injuries are caused by blunt force trauma, and wounds are caused by sharp force trauma usually by a sharp object.

See more examples here to understand that wording is subject to scrutiny.

- Types of bruises, abrasions, lacerations, swelling, redness, pain are caused by blunt force trauma.
- In the description, a bruise is an injury transmitted through unbroken skin to underlying tissue; this creates a rupture of the small blood vessels. Escaping of blood into the tissue with resulting discoloration.

- Abrasion is the scraping of the surface layer tissue from an area of the skin.
- A laceration is a torn and ragged wound.
- Swelling localized enlargement
- Redness is the abnormal redness of the skin.
- Pain is a physical feeling, and it is caused by disease, injury, or something that hurts the body.
- Cuts are wounds from sharp objects. Usually, by force trauma or projectiles.
- Cuts are penetration through an edged tool or instrument that causes the skin to open and to bleed afterward.
- Puncture wound means to pierce with a weapon or object.

The main points to remember when handling evidence is to prevent, preserve, and maintain.

Do you know what evidence can be used against someone? Or you? Learn and discover the evidence that is admissible in court.

The following topics will be explored.

- Hearsay
- Best Evidence
- Secondary Evidence
- Opinion Evidence
- Self-Serving Evidence
- Affidavits and Oaths Taken Abroad
- Evidence of Minors and Incompetents
- Authentication of Electronic Documents
- Non Disclosure of Specified Public Interest Information

Hearsay

As general rule hearsay is inadmissible in court unless an exception applies. These exceptions can be researched on a case by case basis.

Some hearsay can be reliable if the right circumstances apply, and it is within the scope of the law. Since this topic is very in-depth, we will skip this for the sake of this book as this is intended to be for beginners.

Best Evidence

Documentary evidence is the best evidence, so the original documentation is to be produced and precedes as best evidence in court.

Secondary Evidence

The secondary evidence is also relevant in court if the following applies to the documentation.

- The original document was lost or destroyed.
- The original text owns the third party and refuses to produce the evidence.
- The proof is in an official public building, and it would be too much trouble to remove it.

Opinion Evidence

Heard of the saying opinion matters? Well sometimes it does in court.

Expert evidence is a form of opinion evidence. Basically, evidence can be expertly examined and explained in a court. This evidence is considered an opinion where the knowledge is outside of the scope of the judge and jury.

The evidence is admissible, depending on how convincing the evidence is through expert opinion. The individual presenting the evidence will make the difference.

Self-Serving Evidence

The self-serving evidence is introduced to help a witness receive credibility. Usually, when their credibility has been tarnished in one way or another within the court by opposing counsel.

This comes in handy if the person falsified or fabricated evidence and serves to claim their credibility back.

Statements during an arrest can be self-serving evidence as well.

Establishing a person's mental, physical, or emotional state during the statement is another way that evidence is self-serving and can be discarded.

Affidavits and Oaths Taken Abroad

Basically, an oath that is taken abroad is permissible in the courts, but less weight is placed against such evidence as the oath did not happen within the country the trial is being held.

Evidence of Minors & Incompetents

Self-explanatory, but in other words, for evidence to be submitted by minors and incompetents, it needs to be explored before submitting evidence from these two groups.

Once again this is considered on a case by case basis.

Authentication of Electronic Documents

The document that is provided as evidence is an electronic document then the source will need to be authenticated. To do this, you will have to provide documentation on how the evidence was stored or proof that the documents had a secure electronic signature.

Non Disclosure of Specified Public Interest Information

The above in not such fancy words means that the information is not to be disclosed to the public as it may cause government bodies or secrets to be exposed. If you are under the impression that this is about to happen, you should notify the appropriate government body to prevent this or at least notify.

CHAPTER TWELVE

Understanding Actions

Who are you to investigate someone? If you are to act as a Private Investigator, provinces and states require licensing. That means training and exams.

During your investigation cases, you are required to carry your Private Investigator license while on duty.

On top of that, you have to show your license to anyone who asks to produce it.

You are not to carry a badge or a symbol of authority. That could land you in some trouble. Basically, you are intending to be an authority, and that is not allowed, so don't do it.

You are to treat everyone equally and act with honesty and integrity. You cannot use profanity or abusive language.

Excessive Force

Definitely cannot use excessive force. There is a whole section about this and goes in-depth. Determining what excessive force is, that is left up to the discretion of a judge. So my suggestion is, avoid using power if you can. If you have to defend your self for your safety, then by all means, but keep in mind that going too far may not look good on you.

Under The Influence

During investigations, you are not to consume any alcohol or be under the influence of any drugs that could possibly impair your judgment. Meaning that check with your doctor just to make sure if what you are taking could be used against you in court. Probably the easiest way to lose all your hard work.

The above rules come with hefty fines and a possibility to have your license suspended permanently. It is best to think about your career choices if you fall into any of the above categories.

Of course, you could improve and become a better person, but until then, refrain from getting into trouble.

This Is Private Property

An individual is expected to have his privacy while inside their home but not in public places.

Such as a person's garbage once disposed of it becomes abandoned property in the eyes of the law. So feel free to search and seize whatever piece of evidence they may have left behind.

Dirty job, I know, hopefully, it never comes down to that.

Witness Protection

What about people that are in witness protection? As a Private Investigator, some lines need to be drawn, and this is one of them. If you become aware of a person under this program, you will not act upon this information or disclose this information.

People in the Witness Protection Program cannot be pursued as there are reasons unknown for them to be under that protection.

If you are pursuing a person under the witness protection program then ask for help to make sure that the steps you are about to take are within the scope of the law.

Private Investigators cannot act as a Bailiff, collect overdue accounts, and evict people from a residence.

CHAPTER THIRTEEN

Both Sides Of The Law

What is the difference, and how are they being interpreted in law?

Civil Cases

A civil case is a dispute between two parties.

Civil cases are lawsuits that evolve around private rights, injury to an individual, lawsuits against corporations, defamation, breach of contract, negligence, and property damage.

In Civil cases, the plaintiff, meaning the person filing against the other party.

In civil cases, the defendant, meaning the person a lawsuit, is being filed against.

Civil cases are based on the preponderance of the evidence, which in simple terms, means that whoever has the most convincing evidence presented.

The evidence that is presented is based on the person who can convince the judge best. This is achieved by using the truth and accuracy of the information that is being relayed. Strong evidence may not be sufficient evidence.

Even with the right documentation, chances are weighted to the believable person. The person who presented the information without any speculation or twists within the agreement between the two parties.

Much different than a criminal case.

Criminal Cases

Criminal cases are prosecuted by the government.

Criminal law is a set of rules imposed by the government describing behavior that is prohibited by the government.

If you are found to be in the suspicion of a crime, then the prosecution can be placed against you, and ultimately a legal punishment goes along with the conviction.

The criminal crimes are murder, robbery, burglary, assault, arson, driving drunk, and offenses against the public, and society.

Criminal cases are almost always decided by a jury. Often imprisonment is the outcome and may come along with a fine to be paid to the government.

The defendants are protected against the actions or conduct of police officers and prosecutors. The defendant is protected from a law enforcer when he or she violates certain rights. Like the constitution and the charter of the rights and freedoms.

These can be unreasonable search and seizure, self-incrimination, cruel treatment or punishment, and these are just some of the many rights a citizen of each country may have.

Criminal & Civil Overlook

In both instances, one crime can be filed in both courts. One from the government and the other in a civil case for monetary compensation.

The reason for this criminal and civil law are not mutually exclusive, and you can use this law for one single event against the accused.

One can file a claim on a legal basis to seek legal judgment against another party.

Important to understand that a single wrongful act may act as both, a public offense and a private injury, it may imply to both criminal and civil charges.

CHAPTER FOURTEEN

Keeping An Eye

Surveillance is everywhere. Why are we still unprotected from the actions of others? How do you feel when someone is watching you? Do you care as long as you are safe?

Exploring surveillance will give you an understanding that this topic makes the career of an investigator easy and challenging at the same time if that is even possible.

You will get to know how to determine surveillance in different scenarios is appropriate and lawful. You will be able to understand when we use monitoring and how they can go against the privacy act.

Eyes Everywhere

Surveillance is ever increasing in society from the government and the private sector. One starts to question for all the reasons and behind so much monitoring of the people.

The more surveillance we implement, the more people start questioning. Some may construe this as intrusive, to record audio and video of a person's everyday habits, routine, and associations with other people.

Intruder Alert

If the intrusion is not justified, then the person has the right to be felt like being watched. Then the surveillance goes against the fundamental rights of freedom. Depending on the country you reside in, this might can be seen as a wrongful act.

If you are recording an individual, this is considered a person's individual personal information.

Is this the only way?

We have to question the reason for the surveillance. Surveillance is the last resort in an investigation. We may encounter another law enforcer asking us for a reason for the recording. We would have to justify the reason for the surveillance, and we would need to produce compelling proof for the reason. All you have to do is give them the documentation, along with its specific evidence.

One Task At A Time

For example, if a surveillance system is meant to monitor the entry and exit point of a parking lot, you cannot use this system for other purposes without explanation or consent. By providing evidence, you can give the reasons for using the system for other causes. The other reason could be to check employee attendance.

Useful Surveillance

The majority of the time, the governing body will allow surveillance for many reasons.

These are criminal intelligence, investigations that could lead to penalties or sanctions, deterring unlawful activity, and an ongoing investigation.

Surveillance is not allowed when the reason is guesswork. The monitoring of a person has to have a purpose. You cannot say that the video footage is helpful to have or could be useful in the future.

Surveillance in the majority of circumstances needs to be determined to be the last resort. If you can achieve the same objective without video recording, then use that first.

Explore Other Avenues

If, for any reason, we have been using surveillance, when you could have used other means to acquire the same information. Then your investigation would not be considered as viable evidence. Using video recording when it is not necessary goes beyond reason as less drastic measures can be used.

Shoo People Shoo

If a business is trying to deter criminal activity within the area, the other ways are to illuminate the area. Brightening has been found to play a better role in preventing the unwanted activity.

If the establishment wants to place surveillance in their store or outside, an application can be made containing the reason for these measures to the municipality.

Majority Vote

The other more common reason is that the area already has a security concern, and the benefits would outweigh the ongoing interest of public safety.

Consider discussing with neighbors to create merit and reason for the implementation of surveillance.

A surveillance system's access is granted only to authorized personnel. Having access to surveillance and options to playback is to be locked away from unauthorized personnel and outsiders.

If you are requested by an individual to allow access to his or her surveillance, he or she may be given access to view this.

Big Brother Is Watching You

Also, auditors can review surveillance at any given time, and random audio or video footage can be selected to make sure it complies with the purpose of installing or conducting the surveillance.

Unrealized Realizations

Citizens are surprised when they come to realize the work an investigator can do and the investigations they can conduct on someone.

These investigations can be people that are scamming insurance companies for money. Unfaithful spouses, determining an unfit parent, finding a blood relative, finding relatives due to diseases so that blood or organs can be donated. They are checking for arson cases, process serving, etc.

All of which would require a person to use surveillance.

As you can see, given the concern of the public means that to be licensed, the governing body for licensing will need to look into a person before issuing the license.

Perfection Is A Requirement

If you are going to apply, they will need you to be competent, financially stable, and with no criminal convictions. Your the behavior should be ethical in the eyes of the law and the public, and any reason that could affect the general public's opinion, the registrar or licensing agency can revoke or deny you a license.

While you are licensed, you will have to ensure that you are not caught violating any of the stipulations set out to stay licensed. If you are found to infringe, then these can also revoke or suspend your license, in some cases, indefinitely. If you believe an unfair judgment is filed against you, then you can appeal the decision.

A quote to help you understand what other people think about our work and how this affects them;

If all that has to be done to win legal and social approval for surveillance is to point to a social problem and show that surveillance would help to cope with it, then there is no balancing at all, but only a qualifying procedure for a license to invade privacy. - Alan Westin, Privacy and Freedom

CHAPTER FIFTEEN

Ethics Of Law Enforcement

Have you been faced with a dilemma and wasn't sure how to react or respond to the situation?

There are certain times you will find yourself making decisions that can have repercussions. You will need to quickly decide if what you are about to do is ethical.

The investigator will have to use good and sound judgment. In turn, this will help create safe ways out, and if either choice was going to present you with some sort of trouble, at least you will know which one you can handle best.

Tough Decisions

Ethical decisions are tough decisions but nonetheless can be minimized or avoided altogether.

You will learn to recognize ethics in diversity, cultural differences, and contemporary social problems.

As an investigator, you will learn to recognize relevant facts or irrelevant facts and details.

Making defensible decisions supported by facts and research.

Judging The Situation

Judge the situation according to the case and potential dangers. Prioritizing tasks within the case.

Deciding who should have access to certain sensitive information.

Public Expectations

Ethically the public expects an investigator to operate under the rule of law; the public expects the investigator to be impartial, fair, and responsible.

Above all, investigations, interviews, and search for evidence are secondary, and the fundamental rights of the public should not be violated.

The IACP has a great quote and one I like to share with you.

As a law enforcement officer, my fundamental duty is to serve the community; to safeguard lives and property; to protect the innocent against deception, the weak against oppression or intimidation and the peaceful against violence or disorder; and to respect the constitutional rights of all to liberty, equality, and justice.

I will keep my private life unsullied as an example to all and will behave in a manner that does not bring discredit to my agency or to me. I will maintain courageous calm in the face of danger, scorn or ridicule; develop self-restraint, and be always mindful of the welfare of others. Honest in thought and deed both in my personal and official life, I will be exemplary in obeying the law and the regulations of my department. Whatever I see or hear of a confidential nature or that is confided to me in my official capacity will be kept ever secret. Unless revelation is necessary for the performance of my duty.

I will never act officiously or permit personal feelings, prejudices, political beliefs, aspirations, animosities, or friendships to influence my decisions. With no compromise for crime and with relentless prosecution of criminals, I will enforce the law courteously and appropriately without fear or favor, malice or ill will, never employing unnecessary force or violence and never accepting gratuities.

I recognize the badge of my office as a symbol of public faith, and I accept it as a public trust to be held so long as I am true to the ethics. I will never engage in acts of corruption or bribery, nor will I condone such actions by others. I will cooperate with all legally authorized agencies and their representatives in the pursuit of justice.

I know that I alone am responsible for my own standard of professional performance and will take every reasonable opportunity to enhance and improve my level of knowledge and competence.

I will continuously strive to achieve these objectives and ideals, dedicating myself before God to my chosen profession... law enforcement.

What Did You Think of Private Investigation School Book?

First of all, thank you for purchasing the book **Private Investigation School***. I know you could have picked any number of books to read, but you picked this book and for that I am extremely grateful.*

I hope that it added value and quality to your everyday life. If so, it would be really nice if you could share this book with your friends and family by posting to Facebook and Twitter

If you enjoyed this book and found some benefit in reading this, I'd like to hear from you and hope that you could take some time to post a review on Amazon. Your feedback and support will help this author to greatly improve his writing craft for future projects and make this book even better.

I want you, the reader, to know that your review is very important and so, if you'd like to **leave a review,** *all you have to do is click* **here** *and away you go. I wish you all the best in your future success!*

Private Investigation School

www.ingramcontent.com/pod-product-compliance
Lightning Source LLC
Chambersburg PA
CBHW030533220526
45463CB00007B/2809